To My Mother

_____

Brave CREATIVE
FABULOUS Caring
Wild PRETTY
SASSY Nice
cool
funny STRONG
Smart
Tough SWEET
Driven Inspiring
UNIQUE RAD

01

Three words I'd use
to describe you

_____

_____

_____

03

Nicknames I have for you

······ 04 ······

My favorite fun fact about you

05

A hilarious moment we've shared

_____

_____

_____

_____

_____

_____

_____

_____

_____

_____

_____

_____

_____

_____

_____

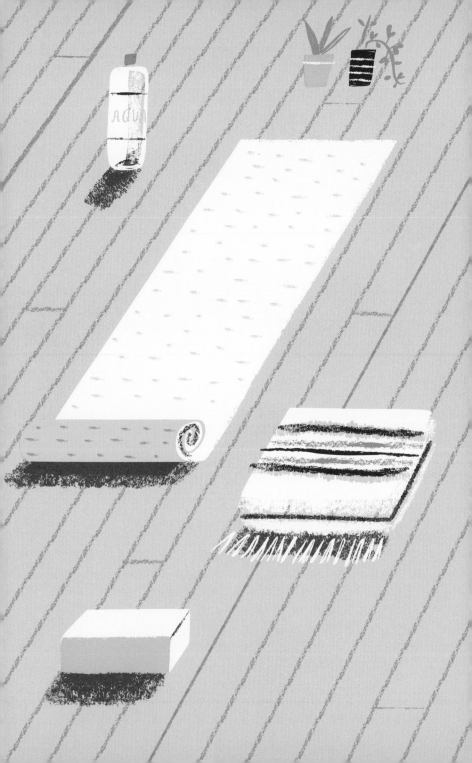

06

An activity that makes
you happy

07

My favorite practical skill of yours

08

Things I know you can't
live without

_____

_____

_____

_____

_____

_____

_____

_____

_____

_____

_____

09

The best story I've heard
someone tell about you

_____

_____

_____

_____

_____

_____

_____

_____

_____

_____

_____

_____

_____

_____

_____

10

Things you're an expert on

_____

_____

_____

_____

_____

_____

_____

_____

_____

_____

An interest we have
in common

A pet peeve
we share

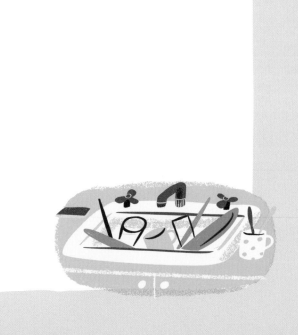

13

A talent of yours
that I admire

14

If you were a superhero,
your powers would be

15

I'll always ask for your
advice about . . .

_____

_____

_____

_____

_____

_____

_____

_____

_____

_____

_____

16

Traits I inherited from you

_____

_____

_____

_____

_____

_____

_____

_____

17

Ways that we're really different

_____

_____

_____

_____

_____

_____

_____

_____

_____

18

A personal quality
of yours I admire

19

When I picture you relaxing,
you are . . .

_____

_____

_____

_____

_____

_____

_____

_____

_____

_____

_____

_____

_____

_____

20

Your favorite hobbies

_____

_____

_____

_____

_____

_____

_____

_____

_____

_____

_____

21

Your favorite foods

_____

_____

_____

_____

_____

_____

_____

_____

_____

_____

_____

22

A time of year I know
you enjoy

May

June

3	4	5	6	7	8	9
10	11	12	13	14	15	16
17	18	19	20	21	22	23
24	25	26	27	28	29	30
31						

23

Your perfect weekend
would include . . .

_____

_____

_____

_____

_____

_____

_____

_____

_____

_____

_____

_____

_____

_____

_____

_____

24

If you were an animal,
you would be . . .

.... 25 ....

In the movie version of your life,
you would be played by . . .

Music that makes me
think of you

27

Something big that
you've accomplished

28

An imaginary award
I would give you

29

A meal that always makes
me think of you

30

A scent that reminds
me of you

A piece of clothing
I associate with you

BECAUSE I SAID SO.
SHUT THE FRONT DOOR!
Hot Diggity!
GEEZE LOUISE!
Slow your roll.
Have mercy!
#!*@%!#*!
OH MY STARS!

Some of your signature
catchphrases

33

What I imagine you were like as a child

_____

_____

_____

_____

_____

_____

_____

_____

_____

_____

_____

_____

_____

_____

_____

_____

34

My favorite childhood
memory of us together

35

A family vacation
I'll never forget

36

A place I'd like us
to visit someday

37

The best birthday party
you threw for me

_____

_____

_____

_____

_____

_____

_____

_____

_____

_____

_____

_____

_____

_____

_____

38

A story from my childhood
I love hearing you tell

_____

_____

_____

_____

_____

_____

_____

_____

_____

_____

_____

_____

_____

39

My favorite holiday
traditions of ours

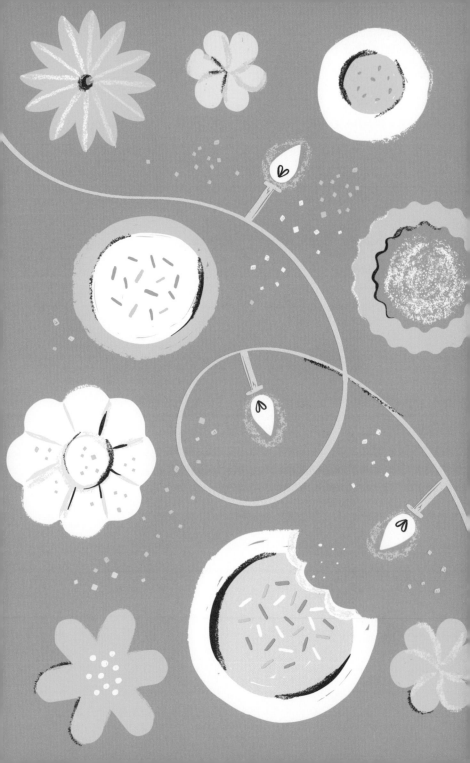

40

Things we used to do together
when I was younger

_____

_____

_____

_____

_____

_____

_____

_____

_____

_____

_____

41

Our favorite things
to do now

_____

_____

_____

_____

_____

_____

_____

_____

_____

_____

_____

42

Something I hope we do
together in the future

43

Things you do that
show me you care

_____

_____

_____

_____

_____

_____

_____

_____

_____

_____

_____

..... **44** .....

The best gift you
ever gave me

...... 45 ......

If I could give you anything
it would be . . .

46

A time when you were especially
supportive of me

_____

_____

_____

_____

_____

_____

_____

_____

_____

_____

_____

_____

_____

_____

_____

_____

...... **47** ......

Something I've done to
make you proud

···· 48 ····

Things you've done
to make me proud

49

Things I've learned from you
along the way

_____

_____

_____

_____

_____

_____

_____

_____

_____

_____

_____

_____

······ 50 ······

A wish I have for our future

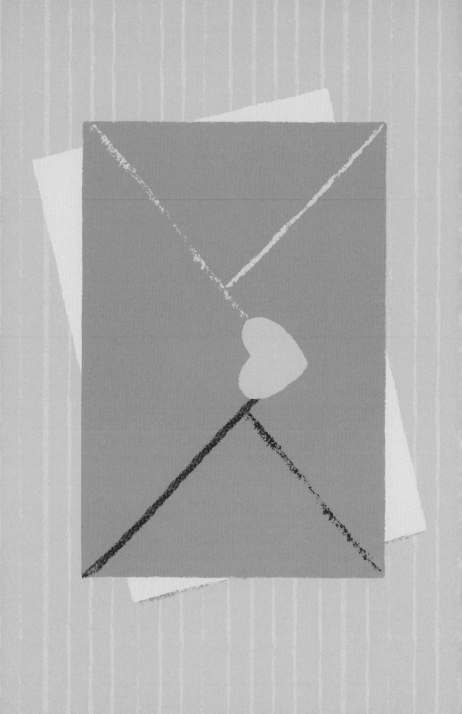

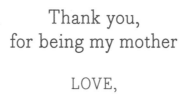

Thank you,
for being my mother

LOVE,

_____

Illustrator: Libby VanderPloeg

Designer: Diane Shaw

ISBN: 978-1-4197-2976-8

Printed and bound in China
10 9 8 7 6 5 4 3 2 1

Abrams Noterie products are available at special discounts when purchased
in quantity for premiums and promotions as well as fundraising or educational
use. Special editions can also be created to specification. For details, contact
specialsales@abramsbooks.com or the address below.

ABRAMS
The Art of Books

195 Broadway
New York, NY 10007
abramsbooks.com